# THE KETO
# SLOW COOKER

*The Ultimate Collection of Quick and Easy Low Carb Ketogenic Recipes for your Crock Pot*

Andrea Adams

Cover designed by Visualarts, contract employee of Andrea C. Adams

This book is a work of fiction. Names, characters, places, and incidents either are products of the author's imagination or are used fictitiously. Any resemblance to actual persons, living or dead, events, or locales is entirely coincidental.

Andrea Adams

Printed in the United States of America

First Printing: Aug 2017

# Table of Contents

*"One cannot think well, love well, sleep well if one has not dined well."*

—VIRGINIA WOOLF

# Introduction:

If you're reading this book you probably already know a thing or two about the ketogenic diet. You may have already been following the diet for quite some time or else you're just getting started with it. There is such a wealth of information out there about how the ketogenic diet works and the biology of what happens when your body is in a state of ketosis. It is fascinating to read up on if you are into science and want to know what is happening in your body on a molecular level, but the purpose of this book is not to give you a scientific education on ketosis, but to provide you with practical tools to achieve your dietary goals.

As you probably already know, the keto diet, in a nutshell, is limiting or greatly reducing carbohydrate intake while supplementing with rich and healthy fats in your diet. In a normal diet, your body takes carbs and converts them to glucose for energy. But when you suppress carb intake, your body needs something else to use for energy so it converts fat into ketones and burns those for energy instead. This will trigger fat loss and minimize fat storage from the food you eat.

Regardless of what your goals are, there are many benefits to the ketogenic diet beyond just weight-loss. In my opinion, the keto diet is one of the easiest diets to stick to because it is simple. You're mainly focusing on limiting carb intake and consuming more healthy fats and proteins. Also, this is not a diet where you must starve yourself. You can eat and be full. You can have rich satisfying food like juicy steaks and butter and dark chocolate. There is a low carb option out there for almost every craving you can come up with and once you flip through this recipe book you are going to be itching to get in the kitchen to try these out.

# The Slow Cooker:

The slow cooker or crockpot is one of the best kitchen tools available for busy people. These days, who isn't busy? We all have so many commitments and we do so much running around. We'd all love to have a delicious home-cooked meal every night but after a long day of work, we don't always have the time or energy to prepare a delicious fresh and healthy meal every night. What do we resort to? Whatever is easy. We order take-out or go out to eat, or we make a frozen meal etc. (or even worse, we just snack the night away).

Indulging in these conveniences from time to time is okay, but the problem arises when this becomes a habit. Often, these choices compromise our diets and we start to lose the progress we've made. I had been trying the "cooking every night after work" thing for years and just kept wearing myself out. I would do really well for a few weeks, then I'd have a busy week and my meal planning and dieting would fall by the wayside.

I had owned a slow cooker for quite a while, but I'd never used it. I had this impression that slow cookers were old news and nobody used them anymore. I also thought the only thing you could make with them was stew or pot-roast and I didn't think the slow cooker had a place in my healthy keto lifestyle.

It all started with the Beef Bourguignon (recipe included in this book).

It was a cold fall day, and I was dying for some comfort food. All day at work I was dreaming about some kind of slow cooked melt-in-your-mouth beef with tender veggies in a rich sauce. I scoured the internet for recipes that would satisfy my cravings and settled on Beef Bourguignon. The problem with all the recipes was the amount of prep and cook time involved. That's when I decided to dust off the slow cooker and see what happened. I prepped the ingredients that night and threw everything together into the slow cooker, turned it on and went to bed. The next morning I woke up to a delicious aroma of the slowly roasting meat and herbs. I unplugged the slow cooker and allowed it to cool while I got ready for work. Then I placed the pan in the fridge and went on my way. That night, I heated up a big bowl of the Beef Bourguignon and satiated my craving. It was every bit as delicious as I had hoped it would be.

From that point on, I was hooked. I couldn't believe how easy and painless the process was. Not only was the meal delicious, but it was very nutritious and fit in perfectly with my keto diet. After that I started experimenting with recipes of every kind. I wanted to see what else I could do with my slow cooker. That's how this book came together. A combination of my passion for healthy cooking and my desire for convenience and more relaxing evenings during my week.

My goal with this book is to provide you with easy and delicious recipes that allow you to exceed your dietary and nutritional goals while freeing up more of your time to get out of the kitchen and spend it with people you love or pursuing your own passions and goals.

Below I have included my top 10 rules for using a slow cooker. If you are new to slow cooking you will definitely want to read these. If you're an old pro, you should still skim them just in case there's anything new you didn't already know.

## Top 10 Rules of Thumb for using a slow-cooker:

**1). Let it work for you:** just plan ahead and work it into your schedule. Throw the ingredients together in the morning before work, or else at night before bed. The slow cooker is designed to save you a lot of time and effort because it does a lot of the work for you. Don't get overwhelmed if you see recipes with a long list of ingredients—often times the amount of prep required is minimal. Sear the meat and toss everything into the slow cooker and forget about it. Your slow cooker is flexible so that you can be flexible too. Don't stress about it—just follow the recipe as closely as you can and don't worry because the slow cooker will do the rest.

**2). Long and Low**—whenever possible, cook for a long time on the low heat setting. Whether this means cooking overnight or all day while you're at work, the longer you're able to slow cook your dish (particularly when it comes to meat) the more tender and flavorful the dish will become. It makes sense right? The lower and more constant the heat, the more slowly the meat cooks, the more evenly the heat permeates the meat. Combining that with the moisture of the liquid in the slow cooker and the meat is going to be falling apart—it will literally melt in your mouth.

Also, this allows for more flexibility in your cooking— it's much harder to under or overcook food in the slow cooker because the heat is low and even. Thus, your slow cooker will be much more forgiving (especially if you're new to cooking different cuts of meat).

**3). The thickening trick:** What should you do if your sauce won't thicken? Your meat is perfectly cooked, vegetables are super tender, but your sauce looks like soup? Don't worry, there's an easy fix!

Mix 1/2 tbsp. cornstarch with 1/2 tbsp. water, add to the slow cooker and stir.

You might be thinking, cornstarch? Is that allowed in a keto diet? In such small amounts, it's virtually non-nutritive. If you use 1/2 tbsp. for a 6 serving meal, you're adding about 3 calories per serving, and about 0.5g carbs.

Make sure to mix the cornstarch and water in a small bowl before adding it to the slow cooker to avoid clumping. Mix it in a separate bowl until completely combined then add slowly to the slow cooker stirring continually. Let it cook for another 20-30 minutes (add more of the cornstarch/water solution if needed), but remember, a little goes a long way!

## 4). Don't over-think it: as mentioned above, slow cookers are very forgiving. If you can't follow the time frame exactly or cannot add the ingredients at precisely the right times in the cooking process that the recipe calls for, don't sweat it. It's hard to mess up a slow-cooker meal so just do what you can and don't sweat it. Just make sure that your meat is fully cooked. If you have to rush the cooking process, make sure to test with a meat thermometer. The following temperature are minimums, but you don't want to overcook your meat so as long as they've hit that minimum mark, you're good to go!

Poultry: 165 °

Beef: 125 °(rare)—165 ° (well-done) (shoot for bout 145 ° in the slow cooker)

Pork: 150 °

Fish: 145 °

Ground Meat: 160 °

**5). No peeking!** As much as you might be tempted to keep opening the slow cooker and checking your meal to see how it's coming along or to inhale the heavenly aroma, don't do it. Slow cookers are meant to be left alone. Try to open the lid as little as possible—every time you open the lid, the temperature is affected and moisture escapes. If you open the lid too many times, your food will not cook evenly and will be more dry. Just leave it alone and everything will be fine.

**6). Use the program settings:** almost every slow cooker nowadays has the programming settings that allows you to set a self-timer. You might be worried that you won't be back in time to turn off the slow cooker. You should be able to set the timer for a determined amount of time after which the slow cooker will either switch to warm or switch off. It couldn't be simpler. Just choose the time settings and forget about it. Prep the ingredients and toss them into the slow cooker in the morning for all-day slow cooking and a delicious meal hot and ready at dinner.

Don't have time to prep your meal in the morning? Do it the night before. Sometimes I will prep the meal the night before and just cook it overnight, then throw the cooked meal into the fridge before leaving for work in the morning. Then all I have to do when I get home is heat it up. Or if you don't want to leave it cooking overnight, prep the ingredients and put them in the slow cooker pan in the fridge, then in the morning, put the pan back into the slow cooker and just cook according to the directions.

**7). No frozen foods:** generally speaking, you don't want to throw a bunch of frozen meats and vegetables into the slow cooker. The slow cooker is not designed to simultaneously defrost and cook your food so there may be issues with your food cooking properly and evenly. Also, when food (especially meat) spends a lot of time at medium-to-low temperatures, it attracts bacteria.

Does this mean you can't just throw a bag of frozen veggies into your crockpot? If only one or two ingredients in your recipe are frozen (like a bag of frozen cooked broccoli etc.) there should be no problem. You just don't want to crowd your slow cooker with frozen ingredients because it will not cook properly. Do not use raw frozen meat (things like meatballs are okay if they are already cooked).

General rule of thumb: avoid frozen foods, but if they are pre-cooked frozen foods and most of the rest of your ingredients are not frozen, there will be no problem. And remember, no raw frozen meat.

**8). Go easy on the booze:** although cooking with wine/beer/spirits can be great and can really enhance the flavor of certain dishes, only use alcoholic beverages in small amounts when cooking in a slow cooker. Why? The slow cooker retains moisture and thus the alcohol does not burn off the way it does if you are cooking on a stovetop or baking/grilling.

Not only can your dish retain a surprisingly high alcohol content, but the flavor may taste harsh and dominate your dish if you use too much since it does not cook down and reduce the same way it does in other methods of cooking. This also means, you shouldn't use cheap brands. Splurge for the good stuff since you will most likely really taste the alcohol in the final product depending on how much you use.

## 9). Trim fatty meat: I know I know. This is for a keto diet—high fat and, low carb. So why do I need to trim the fat? The answer isn't so much for health reasons but for flavor and texture. The fat does not cook off of meat the same way it does when you're pan-frying or oven roasting or grilling. Since the slow cooker is basically air tight and a moist environment, most of the natural oils and fats will be retained. If you are working with particularly fatty meat, you definitely want to trim it otherwise you will end up with unappetizing pools of grease in your dish.

## 10). Finish with flair: slow cooker meals can be on the heavier side, so lighten your dish up with fresh herbs at the end or a squeeze of citrus or chopped nuts etc. Also, generally speaking, you may not want to add dairy products at the beginning because the dairy can curdle if cooked for too long.

Try to add the dairy closer to the end of cooking. Just follow what the recipe says.

## Cleaning and Maintenance:

1. The great thing about slow cookers, is they very rarely leave sticky or burnt residue that takes all your elbow grease to scrub off. Usually you can gently wipe away any residue.
2. Most slow cooker pans are now non-stick, so make sure not to use any abrasive cleaners or sponges. Just use soap and water and either a soft sponge or cloth.

**But what about big messes? What if you don't have time to clean your slow cooker right away and all the residue dries on?**

Usually this can be solved by soaking with soap and water, but there's a trick to deep cleaning your slow cooker that you can try whenever necessary.

**Baking Soda and Vinegar Trick:**

1. Fill your slow cooker with water until all or most of the residue is submerged. Then add 1/2-1 cup of vinegar depending on how much water you've added (the more water, the more vinegar).
2. Sprinkle in several spoonful's of baking soda and allow it to settle as you add more. (follow the same ratio as the vinegar, 1/2c. to 1 cup.) give it a stir and make sure the baking soda is dissolved and then cover the slow cooker

with the lid and turn it on low. Leave it overnight or for several hours.

3. Discard the water and wipe out any remaining residue with a damp cloth or sponge. Wash with soap and water.

# Keto Cooking

Now you're a pro on slow cookers and you can amaze your friends and colleagues with your knowledge and skills. But what about keto cooking? Isn't that really what this is all about? There are hundreds of slow cooker cook books out there, but very few that are focused on your diet and your lifestyle. That's what makes this book different. So often people think they need to sacrifice convenience or flavor and enjoyment when it comes to healthy eating. But that's just simply not the case. It's possible to have easy home cooked meals every night that taste delicious and are perfectly crafted for your diet to help you reach your weight-loss and nutritional goals—all with minimal effort on your part.

These recipes will knock your socks off. They are all packed with flavor and just the right amount of fat while containing minimal amounts of carbs. These recipes will also teach you easy shortcuts to concoct low-carb/keto friendly versions of your favorite meals.

## Top 10 tips for keto cooking

1. **Learn to love veggies:** if you already love veggies, then I'm sure I don't need to convince you. But the number one thing that can help you fall in love with veggies is their versatility. You can do ANYTHING with them. Fry them, steam them, sear them, roast them, bake them, puree them, grill them etc. The best part of keto diet is that most veggies are free reign. Veggies are low in calories and carbs and high in vitamins and nutrients making them the perfect replacement or alternative for carbs in your dishes. If you're in a pinch, or don't have fresh veggies on hand I have a super easy delicious veggie side-dish hack for you.

## Super Easy Veggie Fix:

*1 bag frozen vegetables (cauliflower, broccoli, California medley etc).*

*Italian Seasoning*

*Salt & Pepper*

*Garlic Powder*

*Grated Parmesan (the kind in a can is fine)*

*1 tbsp. butter (optional)*

*Directions:*

*Microwave the vegetables according to the package directions with a few tbsp. of water to steam them. When they're done steaming, add the butter (if you decided to use it) then just sprinkle on the rest of the ingredients and stir. The result: a delicious keto-friendly veggie side dish. (I even eat this for my meal if I'm in a hurry).*

*The best part is, it takes about 5 minutes of your time, it uses ingredients you probably always have on hand, and it tastes delicious—like something you'd get at a fancy restaurant.

2. **Substitute and improvise:** your favorite recipe calls for pasta? Mashed potatoes? Rice? No problem! Just because the recipe is carb heavy doesn't mean you can't

tweak it to make it work for your diet. There are always veggie or keto friendly alternatives. Here are a few of my favorites:

- Spaghetti: spaghetti squash
- Noodles: tofu noodles packed in water (ready to eat, you can get at most grocery stores)
- Rice: cauliflower rice
- Potatoes: cauliflower or eggplant
- Mashed potatoes: cauliflower mash
- Bread crumbs: dried grated parmesan cheese
- Pasta: zucchini noodles
- Rice: bean sprouts and/or chopped cabbage sautéed
- Tortillas and wraps: bib lettuce (lettuce wraps) or low carb wraps

The list goes on. There are so many creative ways to make healthy substitutions in your recipes. With the right combination of herbs and spices and the right flavor combinations, you can make anything taste good. And with the recipes in this book, I promise that the flavors are so great you won't even miss the carbs.

**3.** **Count/Keep Track:** set a goal for yourself and keep track of it. Whether you want to limit the number of carbs you take in or whether you are focusing on some other metric, keep track of it and try to stick to it. It's very easy to say "I am trying to eat low-carb," but if you don't pay any attention to how many carbs you're actually eating/cooking with you may not be accomplishing anything. There are many foods that people consume a lot of and they have no clue what the nutritional value is.

Set a goal or a threshold for yourself and be meticulous about counting the nutritional values of everything you ingest. When cooking, consider everything that goes into the recipe. At first it will seem like a big pain to tally up the nutrition facts for all ingredients in your recipe, but you will get used to it and start to remember the basic nutritional values of the foods you most often eat and cook with.

The great news for you is that I've already done all that hard work for you in this book. The carbs, calories, protein and fat content are listed at the bottom of every recipe.

**4.** **You don't have to break the bank:** many people think keto cooking has to be expensive especially because you are eating more expensive proteins like meat, and cutting out cheap starches like pasta and rice. Just because you're eating keto does not mean you have to spend a lot of money. Meat can be expensive, but it can also be very affordable depending on what kind you buy.

- The great thing about the slow cooker is that it dresses up the meat for you and makes even very cheap cuts of meat taste tender and delicious.
- Pork and chicken are your friends. They're cheap, and easy to work into any recipe.
- Shop the sales—look at what cuts of meat are on sale at your supermarket on a particular week and plan your meal accordingly.
- Get your produce from farmer's markets and stands whenever possible. You can get quality produce for amazing prices at these places. Avoid the big box grocery stores and chains for produce. The quality is usually lacking and they're almost always more expensive.

5. **Splurge when it counts:** it can be tempting to fall back on cheap starches and carbs because they are an economical and filling option, but don't fall for it. Consider the long-term consequences: If you make that a habit, you will slip further and further from your dietary goals. Poor physical fitness can lead to poor health which can lead to expensive medical care etc.

Just remind yourself that you're saving money in the long run. See it as an investment in yourself so that when you're feeling guilty about splurging on pricier healthy ingredients, remind yourself that it's worth a few more dollars now for a lifetime of benefits and savings in the long run.

6. **Avoid low fat/low cal. ingredients in your cooking:** low fat products/ingredients are deceptive because they seem like a no-strings-attached healthier version of the regular version of that product/ingredient. However, low fat products are usually loaded with extra sugars and sweeteners to improve the flavor and make up for the reduction in fat and calories. This means that low fat/low cal. versions of ingredients typically have significantly more carbs than their original versions. Stick with whole foods and natural products. Read the labels and compare. Don't just automatically assume something is better for you because it's low cal/low fat. Besides, you need high fat foods to offset the protein you are ingesting and make up for the carbs you are lacking

7. **Beans are not evil:** many keto-purists may not agree, but I think beans can definitely have a place in your diet. I love Mexican food and could add black beans to anything. Beans are a little higher in carbs and many keto guides say to avoid all legumes, but I think in

moderation they can be a great addition to your diet. Besides having many health benefits, they are packed with insoluble fiber which is wonderful for your digestive system.

Beans are a great meat alternative and they really help fill you up. In the mornings for example, I love to add black beans to my scrambled eggs. Not only does it give them a great flavor boost, but it makes me feel much for full and satisfied, ready to take on the day. Beans can be a great low-cal healthy and natural way to make your meal more filling and keep those hunger pangs at bay.

NOTE: avoid heavily processed beans like refried beans. They're packed with sodium and have lost most nutrients. Stick with plain whole beans either canned or dried.

8. **Natural is Better:** personally, I think using small amounts of natural sweeteners is better than using large amounts of artificial sweeteners. Many artificial sweeteners appear attractive because they are calorie and carb free, but they also contain many harmful chemicals and they are much more heavily processed and not easily broken down by your body (also, when it comes to cooking, they rarely taste very good, baking is

a different story). Plus, some sweeteners have been linked to cancer and other negative health side-affects.

I am a big fan of honey. It is healthier and less processed than white sugar and a little bit will really enhance some of your recipes.

Why honey?

- A little goes a long way. Just 1 or 2 tbsp. in a recipe can make a big difference. Honey is naturally sweeter than sugar so you need less of it to make a difference in recipes
- Honey is more complex than sugar which means it takes more energy to break it down and less of it is stored as fat.
- Honey has nutrients and minerals, sugar does not.

I'm not saying you should use a lot of honey, I'm just saying it can be a better option than using a bunch of artificial sweeteners. When recipes call for large amounts of sugar or when you're baking, you'll want to use something like stevia or erythritol.

9. **Keto dessert is possible:** when you started your keto journey you may have thought you'll never get to satisfy your sweet tooth again. You may have thought you'll never get to have chocolate or eat sweets again, but

that's just not the case. You can still have dessert. There is even a small "slow cooker keto dessert" section in this book. With so many sugar-free and low-sugar options available now, low carb dessert has never been more possible.

And you don't always need to make a whole dessert. If you're like me, sometimes you just need a sweet snack to kill that sweet tooth.

- Dark chocolate,
- berries with whipped cream,
- peanut butter
- yogurt with honey or protein powder—

These are just a few of the simple great ways to kill your sweet tooth. And once you try the desserts in this book, you won't even feel like you're dieting.

10. **Get some gadgets:** invest in a few gadgets that will make your life easier when it comes to keto cooking and it will make your cooking more fun and creative.

Here are a few ideas: (this is by no means an exhaustive list, and you don't need all of these, but consider stocking up on a few).

- **Slow Cooker** (a must for this book)
- **Vegetable Spiraler** (great for making veggie noodles)

- **Vegetable slicer** (very multi-functional, great for veggie pasta)
- **Blender**
- **Standing mixer/hand beaters** (for keto baking)
- **Scale** (weight and measure)
- **Meat thermometer** (get a digital instant-read one if you can)
- **Immersion blender**
- **Grater**
- **Julienne vegetable peeler**

Obviously, there is much more that can be said about the ketogenic diet, and there are tons of studies and conflicting opinions and arguments about the pros and cons and the do's and don'ts. If you listen to them all, you'll drive yourself crazy. Just keep it simple for yourself and focus on one thing at a time and I promise you will make amazing strides towards your goals.

# Part Two:

## *The Recipes*

# Soups & Stews

# Creamy Harvest Pumpkin Bisque

1 Medium pumpkin (butternut, sugar etc) (if using canned, about 3-1/2 cups canned pumpkin)

1 medium swt. potato, peeled and diced

2 carrots, chopped

1 medium yellow onion, chopped

2 c. vegetable stock

1 tsp. curry powder

½ tsp. ground ginger

½ tsp. ground nutmeg

½ tsp. cumin

1 c. heavy cream

Kosher salt

Freshly ground black pepper

Low fat sour cream (optional)

Directions:

1. Peel pumpkin skin, and remove pulp and seeds (save seeds if desired). Cube up the pumpkin flesh.
2. Place pumpkin, potato, carrots, onion, vegetable stock, and spices in the slow cooker.
3. Cook on low for 4-5 hours or high for 2-3. Make sure vegetables are extremely tender.
4. Pour contents of the slow cooker into a blender and pulse until the vegetables are completely broken down and the mixture is smooth and even.
5. Pour the mixture back into the slow cooker and add in the heavy cream stirring until thoroughly mixed. Season with salt and pepper as desired. Heat back up to desired heat and serve.
6. Serve garnished with a dollop of sour cream and toasted pumpkin seeds if desired.

Yield: 8 servings

Nutrition per Serving (including sour cream garnish):

Carbs: 13g, Calories: 125, Fat: 5g, Protein: 2g. Approx. Net Carbs: 8.5g.

# Zesty White Chicken Chili

2 lbs. Boneless, skinless chicken breasts or thighs

1 large yellow onion, diced

1 medium green bell pepper, chopped

1 small jalapeno, minced

6 cloves garlic, minced

3 tsp. ground cumin (add more to taste)

1 tsp. dried oregano

2 tsp. chili powder (add more to taste)

1 tsp. kosher salt

¼ tsp. black pepper

6 cups chicken stock

1 lime, juiced

½ cup fresh cilantro, chopped

½ cup chives chopped

Directions:

1. Throw the peppers, jalapeno, onion, garlic, spices into the slow cooker. Place the chicken on top and fill with all of the broth the broth.
2. Cook covered on low for 7-8 hours. Check the chicken with  fork to see if it is falling apart.
3. Add the lime juice and stir, add salt and pepper to taste.

When serving, top off with cilantro and chives.

Yield: 4-6 servings

Nutrition Per Serving:

Carbs: 6g, Calories: 105, Fat: 0g, Protein: 25 g, Approx. Net Carbs: 6g.

# Tuscan Zucchini Stew

1 1/2 pounds Italian-seasoned sausage (spicy or sweet, whatever you prefer)

1 cup celery, chopped small

3 cups sliced zucchini, sliced into thin rounds

1 green bell pepper, chopped small

1 red or yellow bell pepper, chopped small

1 large onion, diced

3 cloves garlic, minced

½ tsp. fresh ground black pepper

2 teaspoons salt

1 (28 oz) can diced tomatoes

2 (14 oz) cans of fire-roasted diced tomatoes

½ c. water

1 teaspoon brown sugar

2 teaspoon Italian seasoning

1 teaspoon dried basil

¼ c. asiago cheese, grated

Red pepper flakes (optional)

Directions

1.  Brown the sausage in a large pan on medium heat on the stove. Break up the meat with a spatula and make sure it's fully cooked (5-8 minutes). Drain off the grease. Add the celery, onions and peppers continue to cook until the vegetables become soft and translucent (7-8 minutes). Add minced garlic and cook and stir continually until fragrant (2 minutes) Add the salt and pepper, stir and remove from the heat.
2.  Pour sausage mixture into the slow cooker. Add the 3 cans of diced tomatoes, the spices, the sugar and the water
3.  Cook on low for 4-6 hours. Top with grated asiago, and add a fresh sprig of basil (optional).

Yield: 6 servings

Nutrition per Serving:

Carbs: 16g, Calories: 280, Fat: 22g, Protein: 23g, Approx. Net Carbs: 8g.

# Melt-In-Your-Mouth Beef Stew

2 lbs. stewing beef, diced into 1-inch cubes

2 tbsp. extra virgin olive oil

3 large carrots (4-5 medium/small), chopped

2 large yellow onions, diced

2 large stalks of celery, chopped

5 cloves garlic, minced

1 tsp kosher salt

¼ tsp fresh ground black pepper

Salt and pepper

1/4 cup all-purpose flour (can use 1/8c. cornstarch instead)

3 cups beef broth

¼ c. Dijon mustard

2 tbsp. Worcestershire sauce

1 tbsp. brown sugar

3/4 tbsp. dried rosemary

1 tsp. dried thyme

Directions:

1. Season beef with salt and pepper and coat all sides with the flower.
2. Heat oil in a large skillet over medium heat. Add the onions and garlic and sauté for 1-2 minutes (just until garlic is fragrant). Add the flower-coated beef to the skillet and sear on all sides for 2-3 minutes. Be sure to let the meat sit on all sides in the hot oil at least for a few minutes to form a nice sear.
3. Place the beef and onions and garlic into the slow cooker and add the carrots.
4. Put the skillet with the beef drippings back on the burner and add all of the rest of the ingredients to the hot skillet (beef broth, Dijon, Worcestershire, brown sugar, rosemary, thyme).
5. Stir the mixture and make sure to stir up any beef or garlic remnants in the bottom of the pan. Heat and mix until the sugar is dissolved the mixture is well-combined.
6. Pour the broth mixture over the beef and carrots in the slow cooker. Cook on low for 7-8 hours, or high for 4 hours. Keep warm until you're ready to serve it. Garnish with fresh parsley if desired

Yield: 8-10 servings

Nutrition per Serving:

Carbs, 11g, Calories: 250, Fat: 12g, Protein: 24g, Approx. Net Carbs: 9.5g.

# Mexican Chorizo Enchilada Soup:

1 lb. ground beef

1 lb. chorizo sausage (if you prefer, you can just use ground beef, 2c.)

2, (8oz.) packages Neufchâtel (cream) cheese

2, (14 oz.) cans of fire roasted diced tomatoes

1 medium jalapeno, chopped finely

1 large onion, chopped

1 clove of garlic, minced

1 green bell pepper, chopped

1 (1.25 oz) package taco seasoning (or more to taste)

4 cups of chicken stock

¼ c. fresh cilantro

¼ c. shredded sharp cheddar cheese (optional)

Low-fat Sour cream (optional)

Directions:

1. Heat a large skillet over medium heat on the stove and brown the beef and chorizo. Break the meat up until crumbly with spatula. Stir in onion, jalapeno, and bell pepper. Cook until onions start to soften (5-7 minutes). Add, the garlic and continue to stir and cook for 2 more minutes.
2. Sprinkle the taco seasoning packet over the meat mixture and stir.
3. Pour the meat mixture into the slow cooker and add the Neufchâtel cheese and canned tomatoes. Stir until the cheese breaks down and mixes in.
4. Cook on low for 4 hours or high for 2 hours
5. Add cilantro and cook for another 10-15 minutes
6. Garnish with cheddar cheese and sour cream, and serve.

Yield: 8 servings

Nutrition Per Serving (including the sour cream garnish):

Carbs: 7g, Calories: 531, Fat: 42 g, Protein: 28g, Approx Net Carbs: 5g

# Hearty Chicken Soup with Veggie Noodles

1 1/2 lbs boneless skinless chicken breast, chopped into 1-inch cubes

2 C. carrots, sliced into thin rounds

1 large yellow onion, diced

3 stalks celery, chopped

4 cloves garlic, minced

3 tbsp. extra virgin olive oil

1/2 tsps. Italian seasoning

¼ tsp dried parsley

6 C. chicken stock

1 C. water

½ tsp. kosher salt

¼ tsp. freshly ground black pepper

2 Medium-sized zucchini

2 c. chopped Napa cabbage

Directions:

1. Place all ingredients except cabbage and zucchini into the slow cooker. Stir until evenly mixed
2. Cook on low for 6-8 hrs.
3. In the last 2 hours of cooking, take the zucchini and make Zucchini noodles (if you have a vegetable spiraler). If you do not have a veggie noodle machine, take a potato peeler and peel the zucchini, then use the peeler to shave off thin strips of zucchini.
4. Take the zucchini noodles and the chopped cabbage and sauté in a large skillet over medium heat with extra virgin olive oil. Stir occasionally as the vegetables soften and the cabbage starts to caramelize and brown a little bit (about 7-8 minutes). Add the vegetables to the slow cooker and continue to cook for the remaining 1-2 hours
5. Taste the soup and add salt and pepper as needed. Garnish with chopped scallions if desired and serve

Yield: 8 servings

Nutrition per Serving:

Carbs: 7g, Calories: 145, Fat: 6g, Protein: 20g, Approx Net Carbs: 4g.

# Appetizers & Snacks

# Stuffed Mushrooms:

*2 (6oz.) packages mushrooms (white or Portobello) washed, stems removed, and caps set aside*

*1 tbsp. extra-virgin olive oil*

*2 cloves garlic, minced*

*1 (8 oz.) Neufchâtel (cream) cheese, at room temperature*

*1/4 cup freshly-grated Parmesan cheese*

*¼ - ½ tsp. kosher salt (to taste)*

*1/4 teaspoon ground black pepper*

*1/4 teaspoon onion powder*

*1/4 teaspoon ground cayenne pepper*

*1 c. chicken stock*

Directions:

1. Chop mushroom stems until finely minced.
2. Heat oil in medium skillet on stove over medium heat. Add minced garlic and mushroom stems and sauté stirring constantly until mushroom stems are soft (about 2-3 minutes).
3. Once the garlic mixture has cooled slightly, combine it in a medium mixing bowl with the Neufchâtel cheese, parmesan cheese, salt, pepper, onion powder and cayenne pepper. Mix thoroughly until the mixture is completely combined
4. Using a spoon, carefully fill all the mushroom caps evenly with the cream cheese mixture
5. Layer the mushrooms in the bottom of the slow cooker. Add the chicken broth.
6. Cook for 2-3 hours on high.
7. If desired, add more grated parmesan on top. You can also crisp up the tops of the stuffed mushrooms by placing them in the oven under the broiler for a minute or two.

Yield: 6 servings

Nutrition per Serving:

Carbs: 5g, Calories: 100, Fat: 10g, Protein: 7g, Approx Net Carbs: 4g.

# Fondue Fromage with Broccoli

*1/2 lb. Swiss cheese, grated or cubed*

*1/2 lb. Gruyere Cheese, grated or cubed*

*1 C. Chardonnay*

*3 cloves garlic, minced*

*1 pinch cayenne pepper*

*1 pinch nutmeg*

*1 large head of broccoli*

## Directions:

1. Heat wine, garlic, pepper and nutmeg in a medium pan over medium heat on the stove. Garlic will become fragrant, stir and make sure the garlic does not stick to the bottom. Saute for 5-7 minutes.
2. Add cheese to the crockpot and pour the wine mixture over the cheese. Stir to distribute evenly.
3. Cook on low for 3 hrs. If you don't want to wait, you can cook on high and whisk until cheese is completely melted and incorporated, and serve when ready
4. Separate the broccoli into bite-sized florets. Serve raw with the cheese fondue. It can be dipped directly into the cheese, or you can provide fondue sticks for dipping.

Yield: 10 servings

Nutrition per Serving:

Carbs: 2g, Calorie: 190, Fat: 14 g, Protein: 13 g, Approx Net Carbs: 1g.

# Old World Italian Meatballs

2 lb. lean ground beef

1 medium yellow onion, chopped small

3 cloves garlic, minced

½ c. bread crumbs (can use almond meal)

2 eggs

1 cup parmesan cheese, grated

salt and pepper

1 (24 oz.) cans crushed tomatoes

2 (14 oz.) cans of fire-roasted diced tomatoes

1 (6 oz.) can tomato paste

½ tsp. crushed red pepper flakes (optional)

½ tsp Italian seasoning

½ tsp dried oregano

½ tsp fennel seeds (optional)

Kosher salt and freshly ground black pepper

1. Combine all ingredients except canned tomatoes and tomato paste in a large mixing bowl. Firmly stir together the ingredients and then use your hands to thoroughly incorporate the ingredients.
2. Form the mixture into medium-sized balls (about the size of a ping pong ball)
3. Add 1 tsp extra virgin olive oil to the slow cooker pan and coat the bottom and sides
4. Layer the meatballs in the slow cooker and pour the canned tomatoes and tomato paste over the meatballs.
5. Serve warm with extra grated parmesan if desired

Yield: 8 servings

Nutrition:

Carbs: 18.5g, Calories: 153, Fat: 8g, Protein: 33g, Approx Net Carbs: 13g.

# Slow Cooker Thai Chicken Wings:

1 lb chicken wings

4 cloves of garlic, minced

3 tbsp. rice wine vinegar

1/3 c. soy sauce

1/4 c. water

3 tbsp. honey

3 inches fresh ginger root, peeled and minced

Cornstarch (optional)

1/4 c. chopped peanuts

4 tbsp. chopped scallions (green onion)

2 Tbsp. Vegetable Oil

## Directions:

1. Mix together vinegar, soy sauce, garlic, minced ginger, water, and honey in mixing bowl.
2. Heat ½ tbsp. vegetable oil in a large skillet over medium-high heat. When the pan is sizzling hot, sear the chicken wings in the hot oil for about 3 minutes on each side. Make sure the pan is very hot when you add the wings and do not move them until they've been searing for a few minutes.
3. Place the seared chicken wings in the slow cooker and pour the sauce mixture over the wings.
4. Cook on low for 4 hours. If the sauce is not thick yet, you can thicken by adding a 1 tsp cornstarch mixed with equal parts water).
5. Garnish with chopped peanuts and scallions and serve hot.

Yield: 4 Servings

Nutrition per Serving:

Carbs: 11 g, Calories: 248, Fat: 7g, Protein: 31g, Approx Net Carbs: 9.5g

# Spinach Artichoke Dip

1 (9 oz.) package frozen spinach, thawed and drained, or you can use fresh Spinach (6-8 cups)

1 medium jar of artichoke hearts

2 cloves of garlic, minced

1 yellow onion, chopped fine

1 c. unsweetened Greek yogurt

6 oz. Neufchatel (cream) cheese, room temperature

1 c. mozzarella cheese

¼ cup Parmesan Cheese

Kosher salt and freshly ground black pepper

Assorted Veggies for dipping (snow peas, carrot sticks, celery sticks, cucumbers etc.)

Low Carb Crackers (optional)

1. Lightly grease the slow cooker pan
2. Combine all ingredients in the slow cooker and stir until well-combined. It is important that the Neufchatel cheese is soft, or else it will be difficult to combine. Try cubing it if you have trouble.
3. Cook on low for 4 hours or high for 2 hours.
4. Serve warm with low carb crackers and assorted veggies for dipping (a low carb/calorie alternative to chips or crackers)

Yield: 8 servings

Nutrition per Serving:

Carbs: 10g, Calories: 170, Fat: 9g, Protein: 13g, Approx Net Carbs: 8g.

# Buffalo Chicken Lettuce Wraps:

3 large boneless skinless chicken breasts, or you can use canned chicken breast (four (5 oz.) cans)
1 medium yellow onion diced

2 cloves of garlic, minced

1/3-2/3 c. hot sauce (depends on how spicy you like it)

1.5 c. chicken stock

1 packet of ranch seasoning

1 (8oz) package of Neufchatel (cream) cheese

1 c. shredded cheddar cheese

Bibb Lettuce

Directions:

1. If you're using raw chicken breast, place the chicken into the slow cooker with the garlic, onion, chicken stock, and ranch seasoning and cook on low for 8 hours (or on high for 4 hours). If you are using canned chicken, just combine with garlic, onion, chicken stock, and ranch seasoning and cook for (1-2 hours)
2. If you're not using the canned chicken, shred it with two forks. The canned chicken will already be shredded. Add the hot sauce, and the cream cheese and cheddar cheese. Combine and cook for 2 more hours on low (or one more hour on high).
3. Serve with Bibb Lettuce. Spoon a helping of the dip into the center of the lettuce leaf and wrap it up and eat it that way.

Yield: 8 servings

Nutrition per Serving:

Carbs: 1g, Calories: 170, Fat: 10 g, Protein: 19g, Approx Net Carbs: 0.5g.

# Kickin' Mango Jalapeno Pulled Chicken Sliders

3 boneless skinless chicken breasts

2 mangoes, peeled and seeded

1 jalapeno pepper (seeds removed and finely chopped)

1 medium onion, chopped

1/4 c. teriyaki sauce

1 tbsp. honey

2 cloves garlic, minced

1 tsp. kosher salt

1/4 tsp. freshly ground black pepper

1/4 c. chopped cilantro (optional)

Low Carb crackers

Directions:

1.  Peel one of the mangoes and remove the pit and cube. Place the mango cubes and the finely minced jalapeno in a blender and pulse until the mango is fully broken down and the mixture is smooth.
2.  Mix the mango mixture with the teriyaki, onion, honey, garlic, pepper and salt and pour into the slow cooker. Add the chicken and coat with the mango teriyaki mixture.
3.  Cook on low for 4-6 hours, or on high for 2-3 hours
4.  Remove the chicken breasts from the pot (saving the sauce) and shred with two forks. Add the sauce from the slow cooker and mix it with the shredded chicken
5.  Slice the other mango into thin square slices
6.  Build the appetizers by placing a mango slice on the low carb cracker and a heaping spoonful of the mango pulled chicken on top. Garnish with chopped cilantro

Yield: 8 servings

Nutrition per Serving (not including crackers):

Carbs: 9, Calories: 95, Fat: 1g, Protein: 14g, Approx Net Carbs: 7.5g.

# Fiesta Cheddar Meatballs

1 lb. lean ground beef (or turkey for lower cal)

1 lb. Mexican chorizo

1/2 c. almond meal (either prepared, or make your own)

1/2 c. cotija cheese, grated (Mexican Parmesan, you can use regular parmesan if you can't find cotija)

2 eggs

1 (1.25 oz) packet of taco seasoning

2 tbsp. green onion, chopped fine

1 medium jalapeno, diced fine

1/4 c. fresh cilantro chopped

1-1/2 c. salsa, divided (no sugar added)

4 oz soft cheese product (like Velveeta) cut into tiny cubes (about the size of dice)

More Salsa

Directions:

1. If you have almond meal (course ground almonds) proceed to step two. If you just have whole almonds, you can make your own by pulsing them in a blender or food processor until it resembles coarse sand. (2/3-3/4 c. whole almonds will yield about 1/2 c. almond meal)
2. In large mixing bowl, mix together the beef, chorizo, almond meal, cotija, eggs, taco seasoning, green onion, jalapeno, cilantro and ½ cup ONLY of the salsa. Use your hands to fully incorporate all the ingredients.
3. Make flat patties with the meat and place a cheese cube in the center. Close the sides of the patties forming a ball of meat around the cheese. The balls should be about the size of a ping pong ball. Do this until all the meat and cheese has been used
4. Layer the meatballs in the crockpot. Mix together remaining 1 cup salsa and ½ cup of water. Pour over the meatballs in the crockpot
5. Cook on low for 6 hours, or high for 3-4
6. Garnish with fresh cilantro and serve warm

Yield: 8 servings

Nutrition per Serving:

Carbs: 7g, Calories: 357, Fat: 26g, Protein: 21g, Approx Net Carbs: 5.5g.

# Cheesy Herbed Crab Dip

2 (8oz) packages of Neufchâtel (cream) cheese, at room temperature

1/2 cup Greek yogurt (plain)

1/2 cup parmesan cheese, grated

1 Vidalia onion, minced

¼ c. scallions, chopped

½ tbsp. fresh dill, chopped fine

4 cloves garlic (minced)

½ tbsp. granulated sugar

½ lemon juiced

18 ounces lump crab meat

2 large cucumbers sliced in medium rounds

Fresh dill for garnish

Directions:

1. Combine all ingredients except for the cucumber in the slow cooker.
2. Cook for 2-3 hours on low, or 1 hour on high.
3. Serve by spooning a dollop of the warm crab dip onto a cucumber round and garnishing with a sprig of dill.

Yield: 12 servings

Nutrition per Serving:

Carbs: 5g, Calories: 250, Fat: 11g, Protein: 11g, Approx Net Carbs: 4.5g.

# Garlic Parmesan Kale Chips:

1 large bunch of kale

1 tbsp. extra virgin olive oil

1tsp. kosher salt

1/2 c. fresh parmesan cheese, grated (do not use canned type)

2 cloves garlic, minced

Directions:

1. Preheat the oven for 350 degrees
2. Wash the kale, remove the leaves from the stems, and tear the stems into chip-sized pieces. Place the kale in a large mixing bowl and drizzle the olive oil over the leaves, add the kosher salt and the garlic. Mix thoroughly with two spoons making sure every leaf is coated.
3. Spread the leaves over a waxed-paper lined baking sheet. Bake for 10 minutes.
4. Pull the tray out and sprinkle the parmesan evenly over the leaves.
5. Bake for 3-5 more minutes or until the leaves are crispy and slightly dark but not burnt
6. Allow the chips to cool and serve at room temperature

Yield: 4-6 servings

Nutrition per Serving:

Carbs: 6, Calories: 95, Fat: 6g, Protein: 7g, Approx Net Carbs: 4g.

# Main Courses

# Slow Cooked BBQ Pulled Pork

### Pork:

3 lbs. boneless skinless pork ribs

2 c. beef stock

1 recipe Keto BBQ Sauce (as follows)

### For Keto BBQ Sauce (Yield 2.5 cups):

2 1/2 6-oz cans Tomato paste

1/2 c. Apple cider vinegar

2 tbsp. Worcestershire sauce

1 tbsp. liquid smoke (hickory, mesquite, Applewood etc)

1/4 c. honey

1-1/2 tsp. garlic powder

2 tsp. paprika

1/2 tsp. onion powder

1/4 tsp chili powder

1/4 tsp black pepper

1/2 tsp kosher salt

1 to 1-1/2 cup Water

## Directions:

1. Place the pork ribs in the slow cooker and add the beef stock.
2. Cook on low for 8 hours or high for 4-5 hours. Check every so often. When done, the meat should be tender and you should be able to pull it apart with two forks.
3. While the pork is cooking, make the Keto BBQ Sauce first: whisk all ingredients together in a medium pot on the stove over medium-high heat. Slowly add the water until it's slightly thinned. Bring the mixture to a boil stirring constantly. Then reduce heat and simmer with lid propped for 15-25 minutes (until sauce becomes your desired consistency).
4. When the pork is done, shred with two forks and mix in all of the Keto BBQ sauce. Cook for 1-2 more hours in crock pot.
5. Alternatively: you can transfer to a cast iron and mix in the BBQ and bake at 350 for 15-25 minutes.
6. Serve warm. Skip the bun for the most carb conscious option.

Yield: 12 Servings

Nutrition per Serving BBQ Pork:

Carbs: 13g, Calories: 238, Fat: 17g, Protein: 15g, Approx Net Carbs: 11.5g.

Nutrition per serving Keto BBQ Sauce (1 Tbsp) (in case you want to use for other recipes)

Carbs: 3g., Calories: 16, Fat: 1g.

# Slow Cooker Spaghetti Squash and Meatballs

1 tbsp. extra virgin olive oil

1 large Spaghetti Squash

1 (14.5 oz) jars of fire roasted diced tomatoes

2 c. Pomodoro sauce (plain marinara)

4 cloves garlic, minced

1 large yellow onion, diced

2 tsp. dried Italian seasoning

1 tsp. dried basil

1/2 tsp. dried oregano

Kosher salt and fresh black pepper to taste

1/4 tsp. fennel seeds (optional)

Red pepper flakes (optional)

20 frozen meatballs (or use recipe in Appetizer section, "Old World Italian Meatballs")

1/4 c. fresh grated parmesan cheese

## Directions:

1. In a skillet over medium heat, heat the olive oil. Sauté the onions for 5 minutes, then add the garlic and cook for 2 more minutes stirring. Make sure nothing is sticking to the bottom of the pan. Add the fire roasted tomatoes, the pomodoro and all the herbs and spices. Stir until everything is incorporated and reduce heat to medium low, leave for 15 minutes with the lid propped.
2. Cut the spaghetti squash in half and remove the seeds and the stringy pulp (be careful not to remove the flesh of the squash). Place cut-side down in the slow cooker.
3. Pour the tomato sauce from the skillet into the slow cooker, over the squash. Arrange the meatballs in the sauce around the squash and make sure the meatballs are all covered in sauce.
4. Cook on low for 7-8 hours or high for 3-4.
5. Remove the spaghetti squash. Scoop out the spaghetti squash with fork and it will come apart in spaghetti-like strings.
6. Top with grated parmesan.

Yield: 5-6 servings


Nutrition per Serving:

Carbs: 19g, Calories: 247, Fat: 15 g, Protein: 17g, Approx Net Carbs: 12.5g

# Jamaican Jerk Chicken

8 chicken thighs bone in, skin on

1/3 c. scallions, chopped

1 medium yellow onion, chopped

4 cloves garlic, minced

1 medium jalapeno, seeds removed, minced

1/2 cup soy sauce

1/3 cup distilled white vinegar

3 tablespoons vegetable oil

2 tbsp. honey

2 teaspoons fresh thyme (or 1/2 tsp dried)

1/4 teaspoon ground cloves

1/4 teaspoon ground nutmeg

1/4 teaspoon ground allspice

1/2 tsp. ground ginger

1 lime, juiced

Kosher Salt

Fresh Ground Black Pepper

Lime wedges

Directions:

1. Heat 2 tbsp. vegetable oil in a large skillet until the oil is very hot. Sear the chicken thighs on both sides (about 3-4 minutes on each side). Make sure the oil is sizzling hot, but not so hot that the chicken burns. Heat at medium high heat, then reduce to medium when you add the chicken.
2. In a saucepan, combine the scallions, onion, garlic, jalapeno, soy sauce, vinegar, remaining 1 Tbsp. vegetable oil, honey, all of the spices and lime juice. Whisk over medium heat until the mixture is combined and the honey is dissolved.
3. Place the seared chicken thighs in the slow cooker, and pour the sauce mixture over the chicken.
4. Cook on low for 8 hours, (or high for 4)
5. Garnish with chopped scallions and lime wedge and serve hot.

Yield: 8 servings

Nutrition per Serving:

Carbs: 9g, Calories: 322, Fat: 16 g, Approx Net Carbs: 8.5g.

# Beef Bourguignon

3 lb. beef roast, cut into one-inch cubes

2 tbsp. vegetable oil

1 tsp. kosher salt

1/4 tsp. freshly ground black pepper

2tsp. fresh thyme, chopped

3 c. carrots, chopped in rounds

2 c. white mushrooms, sliced

1 large yellow onion, chopped

3 cloves garlic, minced

1 tbsp. tomato paste

2c. beef stock

1 bottle dry red wine

10 slices of bacon, fried crispy, and crumbled

Directions:

1. Heat oil in a large skillet (cast iron preferably). Season the beef cubes with the salt and pepper. Fry the beef cubes—searing all sides. Sear each side for about 2 minutes (each piece shouldn't take more than 6 or 7 minutes total). Fill the pan and work in batches until all the beef has been seared.
2. Set the seared beef aside and add the carrots, mushrooms and onions and saute in the beef drippings (scraping anything stuck to the bottom of the pan) for about 5 minutes. Vegetables should start to soften a bit. Add the garlic, and stir cooking for 1 minute more until fragrant.
3. In a separate bowl, whisk together the tomato paste, beef broth and fresh time until the tomato paste is fully incorporated. Pour the tomato paste mixture into the skillet with the vegetables and add the bottle of wine. Stir until everything is well incorporated.
4. Pour the vegetables and liquid from the skillet into the slow cooker. Add the beef and crumble the bacon on top. Give it a gentle stir to make sure everything will cook evenly.
5. Cook on low for 7-8 hours, or high 4-5 hours.
6. Serve in bowls with the broth. Garnish with fresh thyme.

Yield: 8 servings

Nutrition per Serving:

Carbs: 11g, Calories: 467, Fat: 27g, Protein: 39g, Approx Net Carbs: 9.5g

# Slow Cooked Asian Glazed Chicken Thighs

1-1/2 tbsp. olive oil

6 bone-in chicken thighs (about 1-3/4 pounds), skin removed

4 cloves garlic, minced

2 tbsp. fresh ginger, minced

1/2 cup water

2 tbsp. brown sugar, packed

2 tablespoons lime juice

2 tbsp. rice wine vinegar

1/4 c. soy sauce

2 tbsp. ketchup

2 tbsp. chili paste

1/4 c. scallions, sliced

Red pepper flakes (optional)

Cornstarch and water

(to thicken)

## Directions:

1. Heat oil in cast iron skillet (regular skillet is okay if you don't have a cast iron), when the oil Is hot, place the chicken thighs in the oil and sear them on both sides. (About 2-3 minutes on each side).
2. Remove the chicken, reduce the heat, and add the garlic and ginger. Saute lightly just for about 2 minutes.
3. In a bowl, whisk together, water, sugar, lime juice, vinegar, soy sauce, ketchup and chili paste. Add in the sautéed garlic and ginger and stir to mix.
4. Place the seared chicken thighs in the slow cooker and pour the sauce over the chicken.
5. Cook on low for 7-8 hours, or on high for 4-5 hours.
6. If the sauce is not thick when you check it, you can thicken it by mixing 1tbsp corn starch with 1tbsp. water and adding that to the slow cooker, stirring it in, and then cooking for another 30 minutes on high.
7. Serve hot and garnish with chopped scallions.

Yield: 6 servings

Nutrition per Serving:

Carbs: 13g, Calories: 327, Fat: 15 g, Protein: 34 g, Approx Net Carbs: 12.5g

# Carnitas Tacos Sabrosos

2lbs pork shoulder roast

1/2 tsp. salt

1/2 tsp. garlic powder

1/2 tsp. ground cumin

1/2 tsp. chili powder

1/2 tsp. dried oregano

1/4 tsp. ground cinnamon

1/2 tsp. cocoa powder
(optional)2 c. chicken broth

**For Tacos (all optional, just suggestions):**

Low carb wraps

Fresh Avocado

Fresh pico-de gallo

Cilantro

Sour cream

Directions:

1. Mix all of the spices together in a small bowl to make a rub. Rub the spice mixture onto the pork roast massaging it into the meat. Place the roast in the slow cooker and pour the chicken stock around the sides of the roast (don't pour directly on top).
2. Cook on low for 8-10 hours or high for 4-5 hours.
3. Shred the roast with two forks (it should be very tender and come apart very easily.
4. Assemble the tacos with your desired toppings and garnish with fresh cilantro

Yield: 6-8 servings

Nutrition per Serving (not including the wrap or the toppings):

Carbs: 1g, Calories: 385, Fat: 26.5g, Protein: 33 g, Approx Net Carbs: 1g.

# Eggplant Parmigiana Rustica

2 tbsp. extra virgin olive oil, divided

2 large eggplants, sliced in rounds (about ½ inch thick)

2 eggs

1/2 c. grated parmesan cheese (use the type that is dry and powdery that comes in a can)

2 c. Pomodoro (plain marinara)

3 cloves of garlic, minced

1 large yellow onion, diced

1 tsp. Italian seasoning

1/2 tsp. kosher salt

1/4 tsp. fresh ground black pepper

12 slices of provolone cheese

1/4 c. fresh grated Parmesan

Fresh basil

## Directions:

1. Brush each of the eggplant rounds lightly with 1 tbsp. olive oil and season with salt and pepper. Set aside.
2. Heat remaining tbsp. olive oil in a skillet and saute the onions at medium heat until translucent and softening (5-7 minutes). Add garlic and continue cooking for 2 minutes stirring. Add the Pomodoro, Italian seasoning, salt and pepper. Pour a few scoops of the sauce into the bottom of the slow cooker and set the rest aside.
3. Whisk the eggs together (add water if necessary) and pour into shallow flat bowl. Take another shallow flat bowl and pour in 1/2c. parmesan. Take each eggplant round and dip it into the egg wash coating all sides, and then dredge it briefly in the parmesan shaking off the excess. Layer the battered eggplant in the slow cooker. When you have one layer completed, top each eggplant round with a slice of provolone. Spoon some tomato sauce on and spread it around and then start the next layer.
4. When the eggplant layers are finished, pour the rest of the tomato sauce over the eggplant into the slow cooker.
5. Cook on high for 4-5 hours or low for 8 hours
6. Serve with fresh grated parmesan cheese if desired and garnish with fresh basil.

Yield: 6 servings

Nutrition per Serving:

Carbs: 18.5g, Calories: 354, Fat: 19.5 g, Protein: 26g, Approx Net Carbs: 11g.

# Vegetarian Zucchini Lasagna Alfredo

3 medium zucchini

2tsp. extra virgin olive oil

2 c. Prepared Alfredo sauce

1/2 tsp. Italian seasoning

1 tbsp. fresh basil

2 cloves garlic, minced

Kosher salt

Fresh ground black pepper

16 ounces low-fat ricotta

1 (10oz) package frozen spinach, thawed and drained

2 large eggs

1 tsp garlic powder

1/3 c. grated parmesan

6 slices provolone cheese

Fresh Parsley

Directions:

1. Slice the zucchini as thin as possible—about ¼ inch. (use a mandoline if you have one), then place the zucchini strips on baking sheets and broil on high for about 8 minutes turning once. You may need to lightly spray the zucchini with cooking spray. Remove the broiled zucchini from the oven, drain off any excess liquid and set aside

2. In a skillet, heat the olive oil and sauté the garlic for 2 minutes over medium heat. Add the alfredo sauce Italian seasoning and fresh basil. Season with salt and pepper to taste. Set aside.

3. Drain the ricotta of excess liquid, then combine in a mixing bowl with the drained thawed spinach, the eggs, garlic powder, and grated parmesan. Mix together until ingredients are thoroughly combined.

4. Spoon a few scoops of alfredo sauce into the bottom of the slow cooker. Then layer the first layer of broiled zucchini in the slow cooker, follow with 1/3 of the ricotta mixture, then 1/3 of the alfredo sauce.

5. Cook on high for 2-3 hours, or low for 4-5. 30 minutes before serving, layer the provolone on top of the lasagna. Continue to cook until the cheese is melted.

6. Garnish with fresh parsley and serve

Yield: 6 servings

Nutrition per Serving:

Carbs: 15g, Calories: 364, Fat: 20.5g, Protein: 29g, Approx Net Carbs: 12.5g.

# Easy 3-Cheese Mediterranean Frittata

2 tsp. extra virgin olive oil

9 eggs

1/2 c. fontina cheese, grated (use provolone if you can't find it)

2 tbsp. grated parmesan

1/4 tsp fresh ground black pepper

1/2 tsp. kosher salt

1/4 c. white cheddar cheese, grated

1 (6oz) package of mushrooms, washed and sliced

1-1/2 c. fresh spinach

1 tsp. Italian seasoning

2 tbsp. roasted red peppers, minced(from the jar)

2 tbsp. sundried tomatoes, minced

1/4 cup scallions, sliced

2/3 c. cherry tomatoes chopped

1 tbsp. fresh basil, chopped fine (optional)

Directions:

1. Heat olive oil in a skillet over medium-high heat. Add the mushrooms, spinach, roasted red peppers, and sundried tomatoes. Saute for 3-5 minutes until spinach starts to break down and the mushrooms begin to soften.
2. Pour vegetable mixture into the slow cooker.
3. In a mixing bowl, whisk together the eggs, salt, pepper, Italian seasoning, parmesan and fontina. Pour over the vegetables in the slow cooker.
4. Cook on high for 1-2 hours or low for 3-4 hours. Top with the shredded white cheddar in the last 15 minutes of cooking so it melts
5. Meanwhile, in a small bowl, combine the chopped tomatoes scallions and basil and mix together with a spoon.
6. When serving the frittata, slice it like a pie and top with a spoonful of the cherry tomato basil scallion mixture.

Yield: 6 servings

Nutrition per Serving:

Carbs: 5g, Calories: 234, Fat: 16g, Protein: 14.5 g, Approx Net Carbs: 4g.

# BBQ Meatloaf:

1 1/2 pounds lean ground beef

2 eggs

1/2 c. heavy cream

1/4 c. water

1 medium yellow onion chopped

1/2 c. grated parmesan cheese (the powdery dry kind that comes in a can)

1 teaspoon salt

1/4 tsp ground black pepper

1 c. sliced mushrooms

2 tbsp. ketchup

1 tbsp brown sugar

2 tbsp. Dijon mustard

1/2 teaspoon Worcestershire sauce

1c. prepared BBQ Sauce (use Keto BBQ found on BBQ Pulled Pork Recipe)

Directions:

1. Combine all ingredients in a large mixing bowl and stir together. Use your hands to combine the ingredients and make sure everything is evenly incorporated
2. Form a loaf with the meat mixture and place in the slow cooker. Brush the top with ½ c. of the bbq sauce.
3. Cook on low for 6-7 hours of high for 3-4.
4. 15 minutes before serving, brush on the rest of the BBQ sauce. Serve with extra BBQ if desired.

Yield: 6 servings

Nutrition per Serving (including Keto BBQ)

Carbs: 16.5g, Calories: 295, Fat: 13g, Protein: 30g, Approx Net Carbs: 16g.

# Honey-Balsamic Glazed Short Ribs

12 beef short ribs (bone-in)

6 cloves garlic, minced

1-1/2 c. dry red wine

2 tbsp. Dijon mustard

1 c. balsamic vinegar

3 tbsp. honey

1 tbsp. fresh rosemary

2 tsp. extra virgin olive oil

Kosher salt

Fresh ground black pepper

## Directions:

1. Heat the oil in a skillet and sear the short ribs (about 2 minutes on each side). Place the short ribs in the slow cooker.
2. Dump the minced garlic into the same skillet and saute for 1-2 minutes stirring constantly. Then add the wine, Dijon mustard, balsamic vinegar, honey, and rosemary. Whisk until combined as you bring the mixture to a boil. As soon as it starts to boil, reduce the heat to low and allow the mixture to simmer for 15-20 minutes or until the wine and vinegar start to reduce a little. Then pour the mixture over the short ribs in the slow cooker.
3. Cook on low for 6 hours, or on high for 3. Ribs should be very tender and fall apart with a fork.
4. Garnish with fresh rosemary and serve

Yield: 6 servings

Nutrition per Serving:

Carbs: 16.5g, Calories: 353, Fat: 15g, Protein: 22g, Approx Net Carbs: 16.5g.

# Crockpot Bratwurst:

*9 large bratwursts*

*3 tbsp. salted butter, melted*

*2 large onions, halved and sliced*

*1 green pepper, halved and sliced*

*1 yellow pepper, halved and sliced*

*1 red pepper, halved and sliced*

*2 cups light beer*

*1/2 tsp. dried basil*

*Kosher salt to taste*

*Sauerkraut (optional)*

1. Place all ingredients in the crockpot (vegetables first, then brats on top). Pour the beer over top and add the spices. Give a quick stir.
2. Cook on low for 5-6 hours
3. Skip the bun and eat with your favorite spicy mustard. Add sauerkraut on the side for a low carb low cal delicious side dish.

Yield: 6 servings

Nutrition per Serving:

Carbs: 9g, Calories: 412, Fat: 37.5 g, Protein: 24 g, Approx Net Carbs: 5

# Pesto Chicken with Cauliflower Rice

4 boneless skinless chicken breasts

1 c. pesto (either pre-made, or make your own using recipe provided)

1/2 c. water

1 large head of cauliflower

2 tsp. extra virgin olive oil

**For the Pesto** (makes more than a cup, store/freeze the excess):

3 cups packed fresh basil

3/4 cup grated Parmesan cheese

4 cloves garlic roughly chopped

1/2 cup extra virgin olive oil

1/4 cup pine nuts

Directions:

1. To make the pesto, simply combine the basil, parmesan, garlic, olive oil and pine nuts into a blender or food processor and pulse until the entire mixture is smooth and combined. If you're using pre-made pesto, proceed to step 2.
2. In a medium bowl, whisk together 1 cup of pesto and the 1/2 cup of water until combined
3. Season the chicken breasts with salt and pepper and place in the slow cooker. Pour pesto mixture over the chicken
4. Cook for 4-5 hours on low, or 2-3 hours on high (or until chicken reads 165 degrees)
5. While the chicken is cooking, break the cauliflower into large sturdy chunks and grate it until the whole head has been grated.
6. Place grated cauliflower in a kitchen towel and wrap it tight and try to wring out any excess moisture from the cauliflower—try to get it as dry as you can. Pat with paper towels if necessary.
7. Heat 2 tsp. olive oil in a large skillet over medium heat. When the skillet is hot, add the cauliflower and stir so that it cooks evenly. Saute for 5-7 minutes until it's all cooked and tender.
8. When the chicken is done, slice it up, and place pieces on a bed of the cauliflower rice. Spoon pesto sauce from the slow cooker over the chicken if desired.

Yield: 6 servings

Nutrition per Serving:

Carbs: 9g, Calories: 354, Fat: 22.5g, Protein: 29g. Approx Net Carbs: 5.5g.

# Cabbage Rolls

1 lb. lean ground beef

1 c. fresh grated parmesan cheese

3 cloves garlic, minced

1 tbsp. lemon juice

1 tsp. Worcestershire sauce

1 tsp onion powder

1 c. marinara

1/2 tsp. kosher salt

1/4 tsp. fresh ground black pepper

12 large cabbage leaves

## Directions:

1. Bring a large pot of water to a boil, add the cabbage leaves and boil for 2-3 minutes. Drain the pot and set aside the leaves.
2. In a medium bowl, combine remaining ingredients except the marinara.
3. Once all of the ingredients have been fully incorporated, spread out the cabbage leaves in front of you and scoop about ¼ cup of the beef mixture onto each leaf. Once you've portioned it all out, tuck in the sides and roll the leaves up.
4. Spread ¼ cup marinara in the bottom of the slow cooker. Place the rolls in the slow cooker and pour the rest of the marinara on top of them.
5. Cook on high for 5 hours, or high for 8-9 hours/

Yield: 6 servings

Nutrition per Serving:

Carbs: 5g, Calories: 220, Fat: 5.5g, Protein: 21.5g, Approx Net Carbs: 5g.

# Slow Cooker Chicken Tikka Masala

6 medium (boneless, skinless), cut into 1-inch cubes

1 tablespoons vegetable oil

1 tbsp. butter

2 medium onions, chopped

3 cloves garlic, minced

1 tbsp. madras paste

3 tsp. madras powder

1 tsp. garam masala

1 inch ginger root, minced (about 1tbsp.)

1/2 tsp. ground cumin

1/4 tsp. nutmeg

1/3 c. tomato paste

1 c. crushed tomatoes

1c. tomato puree

1/2 c. coconut milk

1 c. Greek yogurt (plain, unsweetened)

Directions:

1. In a large skillet, heat oil and butter on medium-high heat until the butter is melted and the mixture is combined. Add the onions and sauté for about 3-5 minutes until onions start to become translucent. Add the minced garlic and stir for about 30 seconds, then add the chicken breasts and sear on both sides (about 2-3 minutes on each side).
2. Turn off the heat and add all remaining ingredients stirring until totally combined.
3. Pour the mixture into the slowcooker.
4. Cook on high for 4-6 hours, or low for 7-8 hours. Garnish with chopped scallions (if desired) and serve with a lemon wedge.

Yield: 6 servings

Nutrition per Serving:

Carbs: 14g, Calories: 317, Fat: 9g, Protein: 31 g, Approx Net Carbs: 9g.

# Cashew Chicken

6 medium chicken breasts (boneless skinless), chopped into 1-inch pieces

2 tbsp. Cornstarch

1/2 tsp. kosher salt

1/2 tsp. black pepper

1 tbsp. vegetable oil

1/2 tbsp. sesame oil

1/3 c. soy sauce

4 tbsp. rice wine vinegar

4 tbsp. ketchup

2 tbsp. honey

3 cloves garlic, minced

1 tbsp. hot chili sauce (optional)

1 large onion, rough chopped

2 bell peppers (any color), chopped

1 (14 oz) bag frozen broccoli

6 oz, snow peas (or sugar snap peas)

3/4 c. cashews

Directions:

1. Whisk together cornstarch, salt and pepper in a bowl. Dredge the chicken in the corn starch mixture and coat the chicken cubes.
2. Heat the vegetable oil in a large skillet over medium-high heat. When the oil is hot, sear the coated chicken cubes for 2 minutes on each side. Then place the chicken in the crockpot.
3. In a large bowl, combine all remaining ingredients EXCEPT cashews. Whisk together until combined and pour over the chicken in the crockpot.
4. Cook on low for 4 hours, or high for 2 hours.
5. Sprinkle on the cashews right before serving.

Yield: 8 servings

Nutrition:

Carbs: 17.5g, Calories: 284, Fat: 11.5g, Protein: 26g, Approx Net Carbs: 13.5g.

# Thai Coconut Curry Pork:

2 lb. pork shoulder, cut into 1-inch cubes.

1 red chili, seeds removed, minced (optional)

1/4 c. Thai yellow curry paste.

1 tbsp. fish sauce

1/2 tsp. ground cumin

1/2 tsp salt

2 medium onions, chopped

4 cloves of garlic, minced

2 tbsp. ginger, grated

1 cup of coconut milk

1-1/2 c. chicken stock

Fresh cilantro (optional)

<u>Directions:</u>

1.  Combine all ingredients except cilantro in the slow cooker—mix until combined and pork cubes are evenly coated.
2.  Cook on low for 8-10 hrs, or high for 4-5 hours.
3.  Serve over cauliflower rice (see recipe listed on "Pesto Chicken with Cauliflower Rice" recipe page. Garnish with fresh chopped cilantro if desired.

Yield: 6 servings

Nutrition per Serving (not including rice):

Carbs: 7.5g, Calories: 372, Fat: 27g, Protein: 21.5g, Approx Net Carbs: 5.5g.

# Honey Garlic Salmon

*6 medium salmon filets (or about 2 lbs)*

*Kosher salt and fresh ground black pepper*

*3 cloves garlic, minced*

*1/2 tsp. Italian seasoning*

*1/4 tsp. salt*

*2 tbsp c. lemon juice*

*1 tbsp. Dijon mustard*

*1/4 c. dry white wine (like chardonnay)*

*3 tbsp. Honey*

*1 lemon, sliced into thin rounds*

Directions:

1. Lightly spray the slow cooker pan with cooking spray, an line with waxed paper or parchment paper.
2. Season salmon with salt and pepper and layer in the bottom of the slow cooker on the waxed paper.
3. In a medium bowl, combine the garlic, Italian seasoning, salt lemon juice, Dijon mustard, wine, and honey. Whisk until combined and pour over salmon in the slow cooker.
4. Take lemon slices and arrange around the salmon. Cook on high for 1-2 hours, or low for 3-4.
5. Serve with fresh lemon wedges. Goes great on a salad or with grilled vegetables.

Yield: 6 servings

Nutrition per Serving:

Carbs: 8.5g, Calories: 217, Fat: 11g, Protein: 17g, Approx Net Carbs: 8.5

# Keto Meat Lovers Deep Dish Pizza

1 lb. lean ground beef, browned and drained and seasoned with salt and pepper

Kosher salt

Fresh ground black pepper

1 lb. lean ground turkey

1/4 tsp. fennel seeds

1/2 tsp. Italian Seasoning

1/2 tsp. dried oregano

1/2 tsp garlic powder

6 strips of bacon, fried and crumbled

2 oz. turkey pepperoni

1 (14-oz) jar pizza sauce

1 large green pepper

1 medium onion

1 (6oz) package mushrooms, chopped

1 c. mozzarella cheese

5 slices provolone cheese

Directions:

1.  Brown the ground turkey over medium heat in a large skillet, draining as necessary. While the meat is browning, add the fennel, Italian seasoning, and garlic powder. Break the meat down until crumbly. Add the green pepper and onion and mushrooms and continue to cook until vegetables start to soften (about 5 minutes). Season with salt and pepper.
2.  Pour 1/2 c. pizza sauce into the bottom of the slow cooker, then spread the browned ground beef over the bottom. Pour 1/2 c. of the sauce over that layer and spread. Layer the provolone for the next layer. Then add the ground turkey and vegetables and spread. Pour rest of pizza sauce over the ground turkey layer, then spread the pepperoni and bacon across that layer. Top with the mozzarella.
3.  Cook on low for 2 hours. (for Vegetarian options, you can substitute egg and zucchini and eggplant for the meat)

Yield: 6-8 servings

Nutrition per Serving:

Carbs: 9.5g, Calories: 409, Fat: 21g, Protein: 37g, Approx Net Carbs: 8.5g.

# Mongolian Beef and Broccoli

2 lbs. chuck roast (or sirloin, or flank) chopped into 1-inch cubes

1/2 c. soy sauce

1 tsp. sesame oil

2 tbsp. hoisin sauce (optional)

1/4 tsp. fresh ground black pepper

1 c. beef stock

1 tbsp. brown sugar

1/2 inch fresh ginger, grated (about 2 tsps.)

3 cloves garlic, minced

1 (14 oz) bag frozen broccoli

1 large onion, rough chopped

Red pepper flakes (to taste)

1 tsp sesame seeds

Directions:

1. Combine all ingredients (except the sesame seeds) in the slow cooker. Cook on low for 5-6 hours or on high for 2-3 (or until beef is tender).
2. Sprinkle with sesame seeds and serve hot.

Yield: 6 servings

Nutrition per Serving:

Carbs: 12.5g, Calories: 333, Fat: 14g, Protein: 34.5g, Approx Net Carbs: 9g.

# Mexican Slow Cooker Stuffed Peppers

1-1/2 lb. lean ground turkey

1 large onion, chopped small

2 garlic cloves, minced

6 small green bell peppers, tops cut off and cleaned out (seeds and pulp removed)

1 (10 oz) can diced tomatoes w/green chilies

1/4 c. fresh cilantro, chopped

1 (1.25 oz.) packet of taco seasoning

1/2 tsp. cumin

1/2 tsp. salt

1/4 tsp. fresh ground pepper

1 c. water

2 c. medium salsa

1c. shredded mozzarella cheese

## Directions:

1. Mix the ground turkey, onion, garlic, canned diced tomatoes, cilantro, taco seasoning, cumin, salt and pepper. Mix until completely combined.
2. Spoon the meat mixture into the topless green peppers (make sure to portion evenly).
3. Lightly spray the slow cooker pan with cooking spray. Place meat stuffed peppers into the slow cooker and pour the salsa over the peppers. Then pour the water around the peppers.
4. Cook on low for 6-8 hours or high for 3-4 hours.
5. About 30 minutes before serving, sprinkle on the mozzarella cheese. Serve once the cheese is melted.
6. Garnish with fresh cilantro (and top with a dollop of sour cream if desired).

Yield: 6 servings

Nutrition per Serving:

Carbs: 13.5g, Calories: 273, Fat: 10g, Protein: 27g, Approx Net Carbs: 8.5g.

# Beef Stroganoff over Garlic Cauli-Mash

1 tbsp. butter

1 medium onion, chopped

2 cloves garlic, minced

1-1/2 lb. beef sirloin, cut into ½ inch cubes

Kosher salt and fresh ground black pepper

1 (10.75 ounce) can condensed golden mushroom soup

1 tablespoon Worcestershire sauce

1/4 cup water

4 ounces Neufchâtel cream cheese, cut into small cubes

**For Garlic Mashed Cauliflower:**

1 (16 oz) bag frozen cauliflower

2 tbsp. butter

1/4 c. heavy cream

2 cloves garlic, crushed

Directions:

1. In a skillet, heat the butter over medium heat. Add the onion and saute for 3 minutes. Add the garlic and saute for 1-2 minutes longer.
2. Season the beef lightly with salt and pepper (since the soup already has a lot of sodium you don't need much), then add to the slow cooker. Pour in the soup, Worcestershire, water and butter/garlic/onions mixture from the skillet. Stir until everything is combined and beef is evenly coated.
3. Cook on low for 7-8 hours or high for 4-5 hours. About 20 minutes before serving, stir in the cream cheese cubes until melted and combined.
4. While the beef is cooking, make the mashed cauliflower: steam the frozen cauliflower in the microwave according to package instructions (or just microwave in a glass container with a few tbsp. of water for 7-8 minutes or until steaming hot).
5. While the cauliflower is heating, melt the 2 tbsp. butter in a small skillet, then add the crushed garlic. Saute for about 2-3 minutes until fragrant and garlic softens.
6. When the cauliflower is steamed, drain off any excess water, from the cauliflower and add the cauliflower, cream, and butter/garlic mixture from the skillet into a food processor. Pulse until completely smooth and creamy. Season with salt and pepper. If it's too thick, you can thin with milk or a bit more heavy cream.
7. About 20 minutes before serving, stir in the cream cheese cubes to the beef in the slow cooker and mix until melted and combined.
8. Serve the stroganoff over a scoop of the mashed cauliflower and garnish with fresh parsley if desired.

Yield: 6 servings

Nutrition per Serving (for both stroganoff and Cali mash):

Carbs: 10.5g, Calories: 358, Fat: 23g, Protein: 23g, Approx Net Carbs: 8g.

# Greek Herbed Lemon Chicken

*1 tbsp. olive oil*

*Kosher salt and fresh ground black pepper*

*4 large chicken breasts (boneless skinless)*

*1 c. black olives, sliced*

*1 medium red onion, cut in half and then sliced*

*3 tablespoons red wine vinegar*

*3 cloves garlic, minced*

*3 tbsp. lemon juice*

*2 tsp. Italian seasoning*

*1/2 c. chicken stock*

*4 oz. feta cheese, crumbled*

*Fresh lemon wedges*

Directions:

1. Season the chicken with the salt and pepper. Heat the olive oil in a large skillet over medium-high heat. When the oil is hot, sear the chicken breasts (about 3 minutes on each side).
2. Remove the chicken from the skillet and add the onion. Saute for about 3 minutes, then add the garlic and olives. Stir and sauté for 1-2 minutes longer.
3. In a medium bowl, whisk together the lemon juice, vinegar, chicken stock and Italian seasoning.
4. Arrange the chicken breasts in the bottom of the slow cooker, with the onion/olive/garlic mixture scattered around the sided. Pour the chicken stock mixture from the bowl over the top of the chicken.
5. Cook for about 2 hours on high, or 3-4 hours on low, or until the meat thermometer reads 165 degrees. Crumble the feta over the chicken when serving and serve with a fresh lemon wedge on the side.

Yield: 4-6 servings

Nutrition per Serving:

Carbs: 5g, Calories: 197, Fat: 6g, Protein: 22g, Approx Net Carbs: 4g.

# Chili Lime Pork Loin

1 tbsp. vegetable oil

2 lbs. pork loin

Kosher salt and fresh black pepper

1/4 c. fresh cilantro, chopped fine

3 cloves garlic, minced

2 limes, juiced

1/4 c. soy sauce

3 tbsp. honey

1 tbps. Chili powder

1/2 c. chicken stock

Fresh cilantro

Directions:

1. Season the pork loin lightly with salt and pepper. Heat oil in a large skillet and sear the pork loin on every side (for a few minutes on every side until it turns slightly golden).
2. In a medium bowl, whisk together the cilantro, garlic, lime juice, soy sauce, honey, chili powder, and chicken stock.
3. Place the pork loin in the slow cooker and pour the sauce over it. Cook on low for 5-6 hours, or high for 3-4. Baste the sauce over the pork loin every hour if possible. (if you are not going to be around, don't worry about it.
4. When the pork is done, remove from the slow cooker and slice. Pour the sauce into a dish to ladle over the pork. If the sauce is too thin, you can thicken with 1/2tbsp. cornstarch mixed with 1/2tbsp. water.
5. Serve the pork with the sauce and garnish with fresh chopped cilantro if desired.

Yield: 6 servings

Nutrition per Serving:

Carbs: 9.5g, Calories: 267, Fat: 10g, Protein: 32g, Approx Net Carbs: 9.5g.

# Apple Crisp:

4 Fuji apples, peeled, cored and cubed (pick any kind of apple based on your preference)

2 tsp. lemon juice

1/4 cup almond flour

1 tsp. cinnamon

1/2 tsp nutmeg

1/2 tsp ground ginger

2 tbsp. butter, melted

2 tbsp. white sugar

1/2 c. Frozen sugar-free whipped topping, thawed

1-1/2 tbsp. honey for drizzling

Directions:

1. Place the apple cubes in the bottom of the slow cooker, pour in the lemon juice and stir the apples to coat.
2. In a medium bowl, combine almond flour, spices, and sugar. Stir in melted butter and beat with a fork until the mixture becomes crumbly.
3. Crumble the topping on top of the apples in the slow cooker. Cook on low for 4 hours or high for 2 hours.
4. Scoop out the crisp onto plates drizzle with honey and dollop with whipped topping.

Yield: 8 servings

Nutrition per serving (including honey and whipped topping):

Carbs: 17g, Calories: 145, Fat: 5g, Protein: 1g, Approx Net Carbs: 14g.

# Gooey Chocolate Lava Fudge Cake

1/3 c. cocoa powder (unsweetened)

1/2 c. all purpose flour (use GF if preferred)

1 1/2 cup sugar substitute (use a Stevia-Erythritol blend)

1 tsp. baking powder

1/2 tsp. salt

1/2 c. (1 stick) salted butter melted

3 eggs

3 egg yolks

1 tsp. vanilla extract

1/2 c. sugar-free chocolate chips

2 c. hot water

Cooking Spray

Frozen Sugar-free whipped topping, thawed

Directions:

1. Sift together the sweetener, flour, cocoa, salt, baking powder in a medium bowl. Add the melted butter and stir, then add the eggs, egg yolks and vanilla extract. Stir until combined (do not beat or overmix).
2. Lightly grease the crockpot with a no-cal cooking spray (make sure it is not flavored). Then pour in the chocolate batter. Scatter the chocolate chips evenly over the batter, then pour in the two cups of hot water
3. Cook on low for 3 hrs.
4. Top with thawed whipped topping if desired.

Yield: 10 servings

Nutrition per Serving (including whipped topping):

Carbs: 13.5g. (net), Calories: 223, Fat: 9.8g, Protein: 5g, Approx Net Carbs: 11.5g.

# Slow cooker Carrot Cake with Cream Cheese Frosting

3/4 c. sugar substitute (use a Stevia-Erythritol blend)

1/2 c. vanilla protein powder

1-1/2 c. almond flour

1/4 tsp. salt

2 tsp. baking powder

1-1/2 tsp. ground cinnamon

1/4 tsp. ground nutmeg

1-1/2 c. grated carrots

3/4 c. unsweetened applesauce

4 eggs

3 tbsp. vegetable oil

1 tsp. vanilla extract

1/4 c. chopped pecans (optional)

Cream Cheese Frosting:

1 (8oz.) package Neufchâtel (cream) cheese

3 tbsp. butter

1/3 c. confectioners sweetener (if you can find icing sweetener use that, or any powdered sugar substitute sweetener)

1 tsp. vanilla extract

## Directions:

1. Sift together sweetener, protein powder, almond flour salt, baking powder, cinnamon, and nutmeg. In a separate bowl, whisk together carrots, applesauce, eggs, oil and vanilla extract. Combine the wet and dry ingredients and stir until just mixed. Do not overbeat.
2. Grease the crockpot and either dust with flour or line with waxed paper.
3. Pour in the carrot cake batter, and spread evenly. Cook on low for 3 hours (test with a toothpick).
4. While the cake is cooking, beat the Neufchâtel cheese and butter together (it really helps if the butter and cream cheese are at room temperature and soft) in a standing mixer or in a medium bowl with a hand mixer. Beat until the mixture is light and fluffy. Slowly add in the sweetener while continuing to beat the mixture. Add in the vanilla and continue to beat until there are no lumps and the frosting is completely smooth. If you need to thin it out, use a few teaspoons of milk until at the desired consistency.
5. When the cake is mostly cooled, frost with the cream cheese frosting. Scatter the chopped pecans over the frosting and serve.

Yield: 12 servings

Nutrition per Serving (including icing and pecans):

Carbs: 10.5g, Calories: 351, Fat: 25g, Protein: 15g, Approx Net Carbs: 8.5g

# Decadent Mint Chocolate Chip Pudding:

1/2c. sugar substitute (use a Stevia-Erythritol blend, granulated or powdered)

1/4 c. cocoa powder (unsweetened)

1 c. sugar-free chocolate chips

1/2 tsp. salt

2-1/2 c. Heavy cream

1/2 c. milk

4 eggs

1/2 tsp. vanilla extract

1/3 c. fresh mint leaves rough chopped

## Directions:

1. Take 1/2c. of milk and heat until very hot (but not boiling). Microwave for 1 minute, and check. (if heating on stovetop, whisk constantly and do not scorch). Remove from heat and add the chopped mint leaves. Set aside and allow to steep for 6-8 minutes. Then pour the milk through a strainer into a saucepan and discard the leaves.
2. In a medium bowl, whisk together the chocolate chips, cocoa powder, and sweetener.
3. Place the saucepan with the minty milk on the stove and add the heavy cream, vanilla extract and eggs. Whisk until mixture is combined. Heat on low heat.
4. Slowly stir in the chocolate chip mixture little by little whisking constantly. (scatter the dry mixture little by little over the wet mixture with a measuring cup. Once the mixture is combined and there are no powdery lumps, increase the heat a little and stir occasionally until the chocolate chips are completely melted. (about 20 minutes covered on low heat)
5. Pour mixture into the slow cooker.
6. Cook on low for 3 hours, or high for 1 hour. Whisk occasionally.
7. Garnish with fresh mint leaves and serve.

Yield: 6-8 servings

Nutrition per Serving:

Carbs: 10g, Calories: 350, Fat: 19g, Protein: 8g, Approx Net Carbs: 6g.

# Closing Remarks

I hope you love the recipes I've included here. Not only did I wish to provide you with excellent, creative, and easy slow cooker keto recipes, but I wanted to give you some inspiration to start experimenting on your own.

If you follow the examples of the recipes in this book, you can make any recipe keto-friendly. I really believe the more creative you are in the kitchen and the more fun you have with your food, the easier it will be for you to stick to your diet, and cooking will no longer seem like a chore; you'll actually enjoy it!

Regardless of what your goals are in following the keto diet, you should really be proud of yourself for taking this step. Many people talk endlessly about how they want to get in shape, or eat better, but how many actually take the necessary steps to implement lasting change in their lives? I have every confidence in you that you have what it takes to surpass your goals, and it is my sincerest hope that this book will be a tool that helps get you there.

Best in Health,

Andrea Adams

# About the Author:

Andrea Adams apart from being an author, is an entrepreneur, activist and proud wife and mother. After quitting her corporate job at a prestigious marketing firm in Denver 5 years ago, she started a health food café with her sister, Marta. The café was a great success and has since opened several other locations in Colorado. Andrea only works part-time in managing the business and has taken a step back to focus on her real passion: creating recipes and writing.

When she is not experimenting in the kitchen, you'll find her hiding in a quiet corner of the house plugging away on her laptop—that is, when she is not cheering in the stands at her sons' football games or helping them with their homework. She also fosters stray dogs and helped found a shelter for injured and abused animals. She now lives in Boulder with her husband and three sons.

Made in the USA
Middletown, DE
17 February 2018